Emotionally Abusive
Husbands and Boyfriends

Emotionally Abusive
Husbands and Boyfriends

*Learn about Their Mentally Abusive Behavior
So You Don't End Up Crazy!*

Sharon Walsh Cook

iUniverse LLC
Bloomington

EMOTIONALLY ABUSIVE HUSBANDS AND BOYFRIENDS
Learn about Their Mentally Abusive Behavior So You Don't End Up Crazy!

iUniverse books may be ordered through booksellers or by contacting:

iUniverse LLC
1663 Liberty Drive
Bloomington, IN 47403
www.iuniverse.com
1-800-Authors (1-800-288-4677)

Because of the dynamic nature of the Internet, any web addresses or links contained in this book may have changed since publication and may no longer be valid. The views expressed in this work are solely those of the author and do not necessarily reflect the views of the publisher, and the publisher hereby disclaims any responsibility for them.

Any people depicted in stock imagery provided by Thinkstock are models, and such images are being used for illustrative purposes only.
Certain stock imagery © Thinkstock.

ISBN: 978-1-4917-0878-1 (sc)
ISBN: 978-1-4917-0879-8 (e)

Library of Congress Control Number: 2013917651

Printed in the United States of America.

iUniverse rev. date: 10/21/2013

To my mother, Emma, and my sister Terrie, who have since passed away. To my other two sisters, Linda and Liz; my children, Jennifer, Michael, and Kelly; my granddaughter, Gianna; my nieces; and all of the women who strive to keep their relationships together. To all abusive men, may you learn to appreciate the women who endlessly dedicate themselves to benefit you.

CONTENTS

Acknowledgments ix

Introduction xiii

Part 1. Mental Abuse Effects 1

Part 2. Personality Traits of Abusive Husbands and Boyfriends 14

Part 3. Contributors to Abusive Behavior 29

Part 4. Reasons Why Abusers Abuse 31

Part 5. Confronting Abusive Behaviors 40

Part 6. Protecting Yourself 44

Part 7. Dealing with Stalking Behaviors 47

Part 8. Healing from Abuse 54

In Closing 67

Recommendations 69

About the Author 71

ACKNOWLEDGMENTS

My life experiences have been a challenge for me, but I have learned from them. I would like to thank those who supported me during the difficult times. First, I would like to thank my higher power for giving me the strength, clarity, empathy, compassion, and words to write this book. Without his guidance, this book would not have been written.

Second, I would like to thank those who subjected me to some of these experiences because they gave me knowledge along with the pain. Without these incidents, this book would not have been written.

Special thanks to Almir for helping me get this book published so I can help others in similar situations.

Love to my children—Jennifer, Michael, and Kelly. I am so sorry that I could not be there for them when they needed me and that they witnessed my pain.

Thanks to my mother, who has since passed away, I am so sorry she had to go through the difficult times with me. She proved that I was not crazy because she had unfortunately encountered and witnessed some of these experiences along with me. I am grateful for her support. I love and miss her deeply. May she rest in peace.

I would like to again thank my mother and my sister Liz, who went through the hard times with me. They helped me set up the baby monitor and surveillance camera. Liz stayed up with me all of those nights, trying to catch him. She drove me around to look for my car when it went missing. She watched me get in and out my car so I could make it safely into the house. She helped me carry the ladder into the basement as the police directed. She switched bedrooms with me after the police told me that I had to sleep upstairs. She took care of my children when I could not because I was overwhelmed and exhausted from my leg injury, the endless harassment, and car tampering. I am sorry for the wasted years trying to catch him. I am so sorry that they both had to experience this along with me.

Thanks to my brother Tom, who has since passed away, for installing the lights on the side of my house. Thanks for all of the fun times. I love and miss him deeply. May he rest in peace.

Thanks to my sister Linda, who was and still is my rock. She gave me the strength and clarity when I did not have it. I am sorry that she had to witness my pain. I am so grateful that she stood beside me in spite of it. She has nurtured my dying spirit, which has given me the strength to go on. I thank her for everything she has done for me. I do not know what I would do without her.

Thanks to Alan for fixing the bad leak under the kitchen sink so I could wash the dishes. Thanks for the invites to Florida and the hospitality while I was there. I am deeply grateful.

Thanks to my sister Terrie, who has since passed on, and her husband and children for clearing the snow from my property while I was walking on crutches. I am deeply grateful for their help.

Thanks to my father, who has since passed away, for being there that day and possibly preventing me from encountering a serious accident. Thanks for fixing the wires on my car when they were reversed. I am forever grateful.

Thanks to my brother Bill and his wife, Deb, for allowing me to stay in their home when I was forced to leave mine. Thanks for all of the delicious meals. I am deeply grateful.

Thanks to my friend Lisa, a great friend as well as a sister to me, for being there for me during the difficult times in my life. I do not know what I would do without her. Thanks to her for the many invites out to lunch and all of the laughter she has brought to my life. I am deeply grateful to have her as a friend.

Thanks to the staff of the Women's Center who went out of their way to check on my safety when I could not attend the counseling visits due to the tampering of my car. I am deeply grateful for all of their support.

Last, but certainly not least, I would like to thank the Hatfield Police Department for their dedication. I am thankful that they took my situation seriously and warned me about the behavior patterns of stalkers. They were right all along. The Hatfield Police Department is an asset to their community, as I have personally witnessed their dedication, empathy, compassion, and concern.

INTRODUCTION

Based on the statistics from the National Coalition against Domestic Violence, one in four women will encounter domestic violence at some point in their lifetime, and 85 percent of the victims of domestic violence are women.[1] I have encountered domestic violence abuse in my past relationships. Because I associated domestic violence with physical abuse, I could not recognize the less obvious forms of emotional abuse that I have encountered. Nor could I identify these behaviors as abuse because there were no obvious signs of emotionally abusive behaviors, such as derogatory name-calling.

Although I could not identify this form of mental abuse, I have felt its negative impact. It severely affected my mental and physical health to the point where I walked around in a daze and woke up every morning with aching muscles, as if I had slept in a box. Eventually, I felt disconnected from myself, as if my soul had escaped my body. I was frightened because of the way I felt because I thought I was experiencing a mental breakdown. I then went to see a counselor.

This form of emotional abuse impaired the normal function of my mind—my judgment, perception, and intuition. It caused me to doubt my abilities, inner trust, and experiences. It even made me doubt my sanity. I wish I knew about these emotionally abusive behaviors that were causing damage to my emotional and physical health years ago. I spent years wondering what the problem was in my relationship. Unfortunately, it took me a few more years to figure it out. I've spent days, weeks, months, and years looking within myself trying to figure out what I did wrong, only to come up more confused because I could not find the answer.

---

[1] www.ncadv.org/files/DomesticViolenceFactSheet(National).pdf (May 2013).

Don't let my experiences become yours. Because of the way this form of abuse has affected my emotional and physical health, I feel compelled to help you avoid the damaging effects that these behaviors caused. My experiences, along with the knowledge I have gained from reading books on this subject, which I will include after the closing, have driven me to write this book. This book will help you identify the personality traits of a mentally abusive mate that can be difficult to recognize, which can damage your emotional and physical health. In this book, you will learn the following:

- How to identify the personality traits of an emotionally abusive mate so his behaviors don't end up confusing you. I have broken down the behaviors and named each one as a personality trait so you can easily identify them.

- How to identify nonverbal abuse that is emotionally damaging as well. Encountering this form can also cause you to doubt your experiences.

- How his mentally abusive behaviors affect your emotional and physical health, along with your self-esteem.

- What the contributing factors to abusive behaviors are and why men engage in specific behaviors that have nothing to do with you.

- Why it is not a good idea to confront your abusive mate about his behaviors. You will think twice about confronting him when you read this section.

- What steps you can take to protect yourself, providing an outline of what you need to do to protect yourself and your personal information.

- How to deal with the stalking behaviors of an emotionally abusive mate. You will learn about his mind-set and find helpful tips, including some I have learned from the police, that will help keep you safe.

- How to move past the abuse. I devoted this section to healing your mind, body, and spirit.

As we know, domestic violence surrounds the issues of power and control. Unfortunately, many women think they cause the abusive behaviors of their mates because the behaviors are directed at them. Many will spend years looking within to find their part, only to come up empty-handed and more confused. Many will continue to walk on eggshells and alter their own behaviors to prevent an abusive episode. What most women fail to see, however, is that they are not the cause of their mate's abusive behaviors.

An abusive mate, unfortunately, will also engage in alcohol and/or drugs, which can intensify their cruel behaviors. Many women will try to fix their mates' substance problems, thinking their abusive behaviors will disappear once they become clean and sober. Alcohol and drugs, however, are not the cause of abusive behaviors.

Abusive mates will engage in emotional, physical, economic, and sexual abuse to maintain control over their partners. They will engage in abusive behaviors and then express periods of calmness. Many women unfortunately gain a false sense of hope during this peaceful period, only to be disappointed when the abuse returns. The Power and Control Wheel demonstrates the endless cycle of abusive behaviors.

Good relationships are supposed to be equally beneficial, surround equality, and consist of equal respect, consideration, and concern for each partner involved. There is no imbalance of power in a good relationship. The Equality Wheel shows what parity looks like in a good relationship.

2   Source: Domestic Abuse Intervention Project, 202 East Superior Street, Duluth, MN 55802, 218-722-2781, www.duluth-model.org.

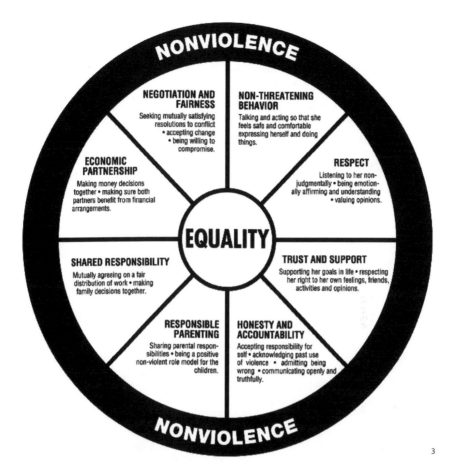

By looking over both wheels, you can see the difference between a good relationship and an abusive one. In an abusive relationship, there is no equality, respect, consideration, fairness, or support for the partner of an abusive mate. An abusive mate will withhold equality in his relationship, but surprisingly, he will expect equality from his partner. The most obvious signs of abusive behaviors are physical violence and derogatory name-calling. Emotional abuse, however, is not only about derogatory name-calling. Other mentally abusive behaviors are not so obvious but can also negatively affect our emotional and physical well-being. This form of abuse is common in relationships, but it is unfortunately not recognizable to most who encounter it.

---

3   Source: Domestic Abuse Intervention Project, 202 East Superior Street, Duluth, MN 55802, 218-722-2781, www.duluth-model.org.

Mental abuse is just as damaging as its physical form. Physical violence can affect our bodily functions, but emotional abuse can impair our mind's normal function. If you are feeling confused in your relationship, it's not because you are crazy. You may be feeling irrational only because you cannot comprehend what you are experiencing. Should you encounter the crazy-making behaviors, you may not recognize them as abuse.

PART 1

Mental Abuse Effects

Encountering abusive behaviors for long periods of time can severely affect your emotional and physical health. Surprisingly, many are not aware of the less obvious forms of mental abuse that are associated with domestic abuse. Those subjected to the crazy-making behaviors without recognizing them will feel the effects. In this section, we will go over the results of mental abuse and the ways it can impact your overall health.

Encountering a mentally abusive mate can take a toll on your psychological well-being. Their mentally abusive behaviors can impair your mind's normal functions and affect you in many different ways. Are you feeling the negative impact from emotional abuse? Below is a breakdown of how mentally abusive behaviors can affect your psychological well-being:

- confusion
- agitation
- exhaustion
- disorientation
- fear
- anxiety
- inability to think clearly
- recurring nightmares

Encountering this form of abuse will cause you to experience confusion, especially if you cannot identify the crazy-making behaviors causing your distress. The bewilderment can impair your thinking and cause you to doubt your perception, intuition, inner trust, and experiences, especially when your mate invalidates them.

Because the abuse is directed upon you, you may look within to find your part in the cause of your mate's behavior, only to feel more confused and agitated because you cannot find your part or the problem with your mate. Mental abuse will leave you feeling overwhelmed and exhausted from over-thinking, trying to figure out what the problem is to ease your stress. It can cause you to feel overwhelmed to the point where you do not even want to think at all.

If unrecognized, this type of abuse will cause you to feel disoriented and impair your ability to think clearly. Their emotionally abusive behaviors will affect your thinking because the behaviors your mate is exposing do not make sense. You will also feel frightened because of the way you are feeling and because you do not know why your mate is irritated. You may start to wonder if a mental illness such as a split personality disorder causes his behavior.

Because you cannot comprehend your experience, you will go out of your way to avoid upsetting your mate. You may avoid him or adapt by altering your own behaviors to avoid the stress, which will unfortunately cause you to experience chronic anxiety. Encountering mental abuse may also cause you to experience recurring nightmares.

More Negative Effects from Emotional Abuse

Their mentally abusive behaviors can cause you to feel as if you don't exist and make you believe that there is something wrong with you and your ability to think, comprehend, and communicate. Because of this, you may isolate yourself from others, thinking they will not understand you or vice versa. Mental abuse will cause you to feel different than you did before. You may also experience feelings of sorrow and regret your relationship, which may cause you to feel guilty. Their behaviors can cause you to feel powerless and hopeless, thinking that there is no way out.

Effects on Your Self-Esteem

Encountering mentally abusive behaviors will lower your self-esteem and cause you to feel as if you don't fit in among others. In addition to preventing you from trusting others, it will cause you to feel unworthy, insecure, and inferior to others, which may cause you to isolate yourself from them. You could doubt your own inner trust and feel less confident. If you cannot recognize his crazy-making behaviors, you may eventually feel as if you are having a mental breakdown.

Physical Effects

The effects of emotional abuse can also take a toll on your physical health and your hormones. You could experience chronic headaches, illnesses, muscle aches, fatigue, and hair loss from the ongoing stress. Emotional abuse took a toll on my physical health. I almost lost the ability to menstruate because of the ongoing stress. Once I understood what the problem was and addressed it, my menstruation soon returned and eventually returned to its normal cycle.

As you can see, abuse can negatively affect your health in many different ways. This is why it is important to learn about these behaviors so you can avoid the damage. Abusers will violate your boundaries. They will damage your emotional and physical well-being and think nothing of it. They will interrupt your peace and sleep. They will tell you what to do, when to do it, and who you can and cannot see. They will even go as far as preventing you from getting an education or a job. They will violate your rights as if you don't deserve them. They will also take away your freedom to choose how you want to live your life.

Conditioning/Brainwashing Effects

Conditioning or brainwashing will lower your resistance to the abuse. The following lists how their brainwashing behaviors can affect you, which can prevent you from seeking a better life.

- **Emotional Dependency.** An abusive mate will lower your self-esteem so you become emotionally dependent upon him. Once he lowers your self-esteem, you will not have the confidence or inner trust to make decisions for yourself, which can prevent you from moving on.

- **Codependency.** Codependency occurs when you put yourself aside to fix your mate's behavior. You will become obsessed looking for ways not to upset your mate, which will prevent you from taking care of yourself.

- **Financial Dependency.** An abusive husband will limit or take away your resources—for example, money, to prevent you from leaving him. He will even go further and limit or deny you from getting an education or job to prevent you from being financially independent.

- **Isolation.** An abusive mate will also limit or deny you from seeing your family and friends to keep you from resources that can help you escape the abusive environment. He will constantly supervise you and go everywhere with you so you have no outside contact.

- **Increases Your Tolerance Level by Lowering Your Resistance.** When you first experience abuse in your relationship, you will quickly address it because your tolerance is low. If you continue with the relationship and the abuse continues, you will unknowingly adapt to it, develop a higher tolerance to it, and accept it as if it were a normal occurrence.

- **Identifying with the Aggressor.** Being exposed to brainwashing behaviors can twist your thinking to the point where you don't even realize it. Should you confide in a family member or friend about the abuse in your relationship and he or she validates what you are telling him or her, you may, without realizing it, get angry and stick up for your abusive mate. You may also make excuses for his behavior. I have seen others actually defend their abusers when many validated the abuse.

- **Effects on Your Children.** An abusive mate will destroy the family unit he has created. He will manipulate and brainwash the children to get back at you. He can also affect the children to the point where they become abusive just like him or become victimized by a sibling. As the children grow and form their own relationships, the abusive cycle may continue all over again. As the children enter adulthood, they may abuse their partners or be subjected to abuse by their partners.

- **Battered Woman Syndrome.** Ongoing abuse can cause you to experience Battered Woman Syndrome, similar to posttraumatic stress disorder (PTSD). The following are the symptoms:

  - **Re-experiencing past abusive episodes.** You experience abusive episodes even when they are not occurring. You may also experience flashbacks of the abuse, seeing images of the abusive episodes flashing through your mind and possibly frightening you because you may believe that you are experiencing a mental breakdown.

  - **Avoiding things around you.** You avoid activities, people, and your emotions to avoid the impact of battering.

  - **Having hyperarousal.** You have a difficult time falling or staying asleep. You will also experience irritability, have outbursts of anger, or find it difficult to concentrate.

  - **Being hypervigilant.** You feel constantly tense and on guard. You feel edgy and easily startled, as if you were constantly in danger.

  - **Blaming yourself.** You blame yourself for the abuse and not being able to stop it.

  - **Holding yourself accountable.** Because the abuse is directed upon you, you may place the responsibility of the abuse upon yourself, not your abusive mate. You feel accountable to look within to find your part in the abuse and a way to end it.

- **Believing your mate is omnipresent and omniscient.** Omnipresent is when you believe that your mate cannot be avoided; therefore, you bend to his will, feeling as if you cannot escape him. You may believe that your mate has unlimited knowledge, awareness, power, and understanding by viewing him as if he were superior.

- **Developing learned helplessness.** You are conditioned to believe that you cannot escape or change your situation. Unfortunately, these are the effects of being in an abusive relationship.[4]

My Experiences

When I entered relationships with men, I was expecting to be treated with equality. I was expecting loyalty, trust, honesty, consideration, respect, and support when it came to my relationships. Unfortunately, I have encountered negative experiences. My past relationships were great in the beginning, but they would somehow take a turn for the worse. I could not understand why I was encountering negative experiences in my past relationships, especially when I dedicated myself positively to them.

I encountered extreme confusion in a past relationship because I was encountering a less obvious form of emotional abuse that I could not recognize. Although I could not identify this form of abuse during that time, I certainly felt its impact, which was devastating because it severely affected my emotional and physical well-being.

I had a strange occurrence from someone in a past relationship. Whenever I expressed my thoughts or feelings, he would alter my expressions and rephrase them to me, as if I didn't have a mind of my own. If I expressed how I felt, he would say, "That's not how you feel." If I were to tell him that he was wrong, he would become irritated.

This person acted like a ventriloquist. If I told him why I was upset, he would not accept my reason and tell me why I was upset. He would verbally identify me as if he didn't know me. His perception of me was

---

4   Source: http://en.wikipedia.org/wiki/Battered_person_syndrome (June 2013).

completely wrong. Whenever I tried to correct it, he would only reject what I said and redefine me as if I were someone else. For some reason, he could not acknowledge me, which caused me to feel as if I were invisible.

Not only did he not recognize me, he couldn't identify himself. If I confronted him about something he had said, he would tell me that he never said it, I was imagining things or hearing voices that weren't his, or I was crazy.

He would also accuse me of doing things I did not do. One day, I went to lunch with a friend. I opened my wallet to pay for my meal and then realized that I did not have enough money to pay for it. I borrowed the money from my friend to pay for my lunch and returned it to her the next day. Later that evening, I asked if he had taken money out of my wallet. He denied it and then told me that I might have spent it without realizing it. Because I trusted him, I doubted myself, thinking I might have done what he said.

Another day, he approached me and showed me letters from the bank about checks I had written that had bounced. He then accused me of taking money out of the account. I looked over the checkbook but couldn't find the problem. He then grabbed the checkbook from me and told me that he would handle the finances. When I defended myself against his accusations, he accused me of attacking and abusing him. Was I going insane?

Did I really do these things that I was being accused of, or am I crazy because I don't remember doing them? Was I really encountering these experiences, or am I imagining them because he denied my experiences? Because I didn't understand what I was encountering, I decided to withdraw emotionally to ease my stress and to see if I had a part in the cause of his behavior. To my surprise, he continued the behavior even though I wasn't emotionally present. I then realized that I wasn't the problem and ended the relationship shortly thereafter.

My past experiences so confused me that I couldn't think straight. I went to see a counselor because I felt extremely confused and didn't know why. Not only was I suffering from extreme confusion in my past relationship, a man I did not know was stalking me.

Stalked

In early 1992, a man I did not know stalked me. The stalking incidents began in the winter, just two months after I moved into a new neighborhood. My youngest of three had just turned three months old. This stalker began knocking at the front door around three o'clock in the morning. At first, I thought it was just kids playing around until it happened again and again. I called the police, but nothing could be done because I could not identify the person who was causing the harassment.

Being alone in the suburbs with three small children and being harassed by a man I did not even know was very frightening. Because my extended family members lived an hour away from me, my mother and sister decided to move in with me because they were worried about my safety. This stalker would randomly knock on the front door in the middle of the night, three to four times a week.

Desperate to end the harassment, I set up a surveillance camera and hooked it up to my video recorder. I set up the camera to record his activity by the front door. I also used a baby monitor and hid it in the bushes next to the front door so the sound of his presence could alert me when I was asleep. I set the video timer to record all night, hoping to get his identity on tape by dawn. To my surprise, this stalker began knocking at the opposite end of the house, as if to tell me that he was watching everything I did inside of my house.

While I was brushing my teeth in the master bedroom bath one night, I heard this stalker walking on the back deck. Hearing the sound of his footsteps get louder and louder as he approached the window, I quickly ran out of the room and screamed for my mother to call the police. While I was getting my three-year-old ready for bed one night, I stepped out of the bedroom for a minute. All of a sudden, my youngest one began screaming. I ran back into the room and saw my daughter pointing to the window, screaming the words, "Bad man, Mom! Like door! Like door." I was so angry that I quickly opened the front door, stepped outside, and began yelling at this stalker even though I couldn't see him.

Another night, I woke up to the sound of the dog barking at the bedroom window around three o'clock in the morning. Stirring out of sleep, facing the window, I quickly opened my eyes only to find this stalker, just inches from my face looking at me through the bedroom window. I was so frightened that I could not move. Unfortunately, I had a leg injury during this time, and I was walking with crutches along with a locked leg brace. I quickly collected myself, grabbed my crutches, and quickly got out of the bedroom, screaming for my mother to call the police. The police arrived and then told me that I would have to move up to a second-floor bedroom. My bedroom was on the first floor. Because of my leg injury, I had to sit and pull myself up each step to get up to the second floor. I also had to sit and slide down each step to get back down to the first floor. I had to go up and down the stairs like this for nearly fourteen weeks.

As daylight savings time approached, I thought it would be safe to have my nephew spend the night at my house. My nephew and son slept on the floor in the family room. I decided to sleep on the sofa to watch over them. Our dog Tasha decided to sleep in the family room with us. A few hours later, I woke up to the sound of the dog barking by the family room door. I quickly opened my eyes, only to see this stalker trying to break in. With my fear overwhelming me, I quickly got the boys out of the room and screamed for my mother and sister to call the police. After that, I could not allow anyone to sleep over at our house.

I was cleaning up the kitchen after dinner one day. I collected the recyclables for my son to take out to the recyclable can, which was located on the right side of the house. After I finished cleaning up the kitchen, I sat down to read a book. My son did what I asked and then quickly came back in, extremely upset, while locking the front door. With fear overwhelming him, he told me that a man was looking at me through the kitchen window. I quickly moved away from the window and called the police. The police arrived shortly thereafter and questioned my son about this man's identity. My son told the police that he couldn't identify the man because he blocked his face and ran when he saw him. My son, however, was able to identify what he was wearing.

While my daughter and I were walking the dogs one night out in the front yard because it wasn't safe to walk them out in the backyard, the stalker suddenly threw a rock in our direction. It fortunately missed us and hit the corner of the house. The sound of the rock hitting the aluminum siding alerted me of his presence, and my daughter and I quickly ran back into the house, locked the doors, and called the police.

Not only was I dealing with the stalker knocking on my front door and windows throughout the first floor, someone began tampering with my car. One day, I took my mother to the store, which was about two miles from her house. As I was driving, I pressed on the brake pedal to slow down for an approaching stop sign. As I pressed down, I quickly realized that the brakes were not working, and panic set in as my car coasted through the stop sign.

Another morning, I drove to the store, which was less than a mile away from my house, to get milk. As I was driving back from the store, I tried to slow down to make a left-hand turn onto my street and quickly realized that I had no brakes. Panic set in once again as I coasted the car down the street and into my driveway.

Another afternoon, I drove to my brother's house to see my father, who was visiting from Florida. As I was leaving my brother's house, my father walked me out to my car. He then walked to the back of my car to help me back out of the parking space. As he was watching me back up, he noticed wires hanging from the trunk and then told me to stop the car.

My father then asked me to turn on the right and left turn signals. When I turned on the left turn signal, the right signal would flash. When I turned on the right signal, the left one would flash. My father then told me that someone had reversed the wires on my car. He then asked me to open the trunk so he could fix the wires. Fortunately, my father was a mechanic and able to fix it.

With stress overwhelming me, I called my counselor about my situation and made an appointment to see her. I went to a few visits and then had to cancel because someone had sliced the hoses on my car. My counselor then arranged for me to have my sessions by phone because my driving days were limited.

Not only was I dealing with the loud knocks on my doors and windows, car problems, and a stalker trying to break in my house, I was also getting strange phone calls. One day, a woman called me from a cemetery company and told me that someone had called them and said I needed a burial plot. The woman then told me that my plot was ready. She told me that she was so sorry that I needed a burial plot so soon and then asked me if I were terminally ill. I then told her that I wasn't sick.

As she was listening to me speak, she said I sounded too young to need a burial plot. She then asked me how old I was. I responded and then asked if she knew the name of the person who had contacted her. She told me that she received a call from someone, but he didn't leave his name. She then apologized for the call. A few months later, I received another call that was similar to this one.

This stalker harassed me for nearly six years. I had to eventually move out of my home because it was getting too dangerous to stay. For years, I could hear him whistling as he was lurking around my house at night, but I could never see him because it was too dark. During the fall and winter months, I could hear the crackling sounds of the leaves and snow as he walked closer and closer to my house. Unfortunately, I never found out his identity.

Emotional Abuse

I also experienced another form of emotional abuse in another past relationship. This person would deliberately antagonize me to provoke me to anger. For example, he would block my view of the television. When I asked him to move, he refused until I became angry enough to the point where I had to get up from the sofa to leave the room. He would also refuse to answer my questions. When I would ask a question about something, he would ignore me and look past me as if I weren't there. When I confronted him about his behavior, he would ignore me or go to another room, lock the door, and say he needed protection from me.

Conclusion

I did not understand why these experiences occurred in my past relationships, but they did in spite of my dedication. During the time when my driving days were limited, I began writing to try to make sense of my experiences, unbeknownst that the pen and paper would become my best friend.

Remember the lunch money story? He was taking money out of my wallet without my knowledge. Someone caught him one day and told me. Remember when he accused me of taking money out of the account? He was taking out blank checks near the back of the checkbook so I wouldn't notice. He used these blank checks to open six bank accounts. When I questioned him about these six accounts, his response was that I was missing one.

I then realized that I wasn't crazy after all. I eventually became aware that those in my past relationships were accusing me of doing things that they were doing. An abusive mate can maintain control over you by leading you into thinking that you are crazy. If your mate continuously tells you that you are crazy, he may be the one who's causing you to feel crazy in the first place.

Does your mate act as if you are hiding something from him? Does he tell you that you are crazy? Does he accuse you of doing things you're not? Does he refuse to answer your questions? Does he act as if you do not exist? Does he reject your expressions? Does he deny what he says to you? Does he identify you as if he never knew you? Does he become irritated when you confront him about his behavior? Can you answer yes to some of the questions above? If you can, then you may be experiencing the crazy-making forms of emotional abuse.

The movie *Gaslight* demonstrates the effects of the crazy-making behaviors very well. Filmed in 1944, this movie surrounds the ongoing emotional abuse of a dedicated wife. The husband was taking and moving things around the house and would then accuse his wife of his actions. The wife became emotionally unstable soon after her husband began accusing her of taking and moving things out of place without remembering. He would tell her that she was crazy. Because she trusted her husband, she started to believe that she was actually going insane.

Gaslight demonstrates how emotional abuse can alter our state of mind, perceptions, and experiences and cause us to doubt the truth. Emotional abuse violates our trust, causes us to doubt our intuition and judgment, and impairs our ability to think clearly. This crazy-making form of abuse needs more exposure because many women have (and many will continue) to suffer in silence because they cannot comprehend, identify, or explain their experiences to others to end their misery.

Our experiences provoke our feelings. For example, experiences such as winning a prize, getting a new car, riding on a roller coaster, or receiving a gift provoke feelings of joy. We can also encounter incidents from people and experience certain feelings from others' personalities. People are an experience because they can also affect our feelings. The experiences we get from people, however, can be more difficult to comprehend and identify.

It is easier to recognize the experience of a roller-coaster ride than it is to identify the experience of one's complex personality. In order to comprehend our experience, we must identify its source. That will help us prevent confusion. If a doctor cannot identify an illness, he or she cannot treat it. Similarly, if we cannot comprehend or identify the source that is causing our confusion, we cannot end our confusion.

PART 2

Personality Traits of Abusive Husbands and Boyfriends

To identify the personality traits of an abusive husband or an abusive boyfriend, you need to recognize the confusing behaviors of emotional and nonverbal abuse. Because some forms of emotional abuse have puzzled so many, I will finally expose these bewildering emotionally abusive behaviors and categorize them under specific abusive personality traits, which I have named, so you can identify them should you encounter them in your relationship.

The Bully

Does your mate pick a fight with you without cause?
Does he invade your personal space?
Does he force you to do as he wishes?
Does he physically intimidate you?
Is he unwilling to compromise?
Does he constantly complain?
Does he shove or push you?
Does he hate to lose?
Is he overly sensitive?
Is he quick to temper?
Does he challenge your physical power?
Does he come up close to your face when you are speaking?
Does he block you from entering or leaving a room?
Does he bump into you or throw things and then claim it was an accident?

If you are encountering some of the above behaviors, chances are, the bully has found his way into your home. Some bullies unfortunately just grow bigger and will target women and children because of their imbalance of physical power. The adult bully acts just like the child bully, only he is bigger and physically stronger, and he may throw a tantrum if he doesn't get his way. He is sensitive to criticism and quick to show his temper. He does not take jokes in a flippant manner. He does not like to compromise. "It's his way or the highway." The bully doesn't like to lose, whether he is playing a game or engaging in a conversation.

The bully will abuse his physical power in not so obvious ways to make it appear as if his behavior weren't deliberate. He will invade your personal space. He will periodically bump into you or throw something in your direction and then claim it was an accident. He may surprisingly jump out of nowhere to startle you and then claim he was just joking. He will also come up close to your face if you differ in opinion.

You may have to fight for peace if you have encountered the bully. Like the child bully, the adult bully will pick a fight with you without cause. He will abuse his physical power and engage in pushing and shoving. He will constantly challenge your physical power. Should you walk away from his behavior, he will physically block you from entering or leaving a room and ask, "What are you going to do about it?" He knows that you cannot physically move him out of the way, but he may challenge you to do so anyway.

The Corrections Officer

Do you feel as if you can't do anything right?
Does he make condescending remarks about you?
Does he comment on the way you walk, sit, speak, or eat?
Does he correct your grammar?
Does he make you feel self-conscious?
Does he point out your imperfections?

Does he mock the behaviors of others, including you?
Does it seem like he's watching every move you make?
Does he make suggestions on how you can improve yourself?

If you are experiencing some of these behaviors, then you may already know that you are living in a boot camp with a corrections officer. He will sentence you and the children to life in a boot camp. He is not officially a corrections officer, but he sure knows how to act like one. Even if he were a corrections officer, his behaviors do not belong in the home.

The corrections officer will first take note of your physical appearance, such as your weight, teeth, hair, and any markings on your body, and then will watch the way you walk, dress, eat, and sleep. He will then take note of your personality, such as the way you speak, the tone of your voice, and the way you express yourself to others.

Once he has analyzed your physical appearance and personality, he will begin to make condescending remarks about them, as if they were all wrong. He will comment about your weight and your crooked tooth and may jokingly point out any markings on your skin, such as scars or other imperfections. He will even correct your grammar. He will then give you suggestions on how you can improve yourself.

The corrections officer may not stop here. He may also extend his behaviors to your family members and friends. He will become irritated if you and/or the children fall short of what he finds acceptable. He may make negative comments about you in a deceptive manner, acting as if he is trying to support you. His kind criticisms, however, may be a less obvious way to lower your self-esteem. If you are feeling worthy and confident, you can be sure that he will find a way to take away these feelings with his constant criticisms and suggestions on how you can improve yourself.

Prison Warden

Does your mate screen your phone calls?
Does he time your outside activities?
Does he accuse you of having an affair?
Does he act as if he doesn't trust you?
Does he act paranoid?
Does he verbally threaten you?
Does he control all the finances?
Does he take away the car keys when he is angry?
Does he physically abuse or intimidate you?
Does he limit or deny you monetary access?
Does he act as if you are hiding something from him?
Does he limit or prevent you from family and friends?
Does he prevent you from working or getting an education?

Can you answer yes to some of these questions? If so, chances are, you are dealing with a prison warden who will make you his POW. He will charm you into a relationship and then secretly trap you by making it difficult for you to escape. He will push for a quick marriage or pregnancy and then limit or take away your resources. Once he takes away your means, he will begin to subject you to his abusive behaviors.

The prison warden will direct his abuse upon you, which will cause you to become distant. Once he senses that you are avoiding him, he will begin to act suspicious as if you are hiding something from him. Because he is suspicious, he may begin screening your phone calls and will question any calls that were made to and from you. He will eventually accuse you of having an affair. He will view your distance as a sign that you are planning to abandon him, and he may become obsessed with preventing you from leaving to maintain his control over you.

Because the prison warden is suspicious about your distance, he may limit and time your outside activities, along with your encounters with family and friends. He will also prevent you from getting an education or working outside the home. Once you have had enough of his behavior and tell him that you want to end the relationship, he may increase his abusive actions to prevent you from leaving. He unfortunately will increase his abuse to physical mistreatment if he senses he is losing control over you.

King of the Castle

Does your mate show sexist behavior?
Do you feel like a servant?
Does he treat you like a subordinate?
Does he tell you what to do?
Does he demand perfection?
Does he withhold his feelings?
Does he plan how you spend your day?
Do you feel as if you do not have time for yourself?
Does he get upset if things are moved out of place?

Does he get upset if things don't go as planned?
Does he make you ask permission for money or to do anything?

Can you answer yes to some of the questions above? If so, chances are, you are with the king of the castle. He feels privileged to treat you as a servant because of his sexist belief that women are here only to serve him. The king of the castle will trap you into servitude. Slavery unfortunately still exists behind the closed doors of many homes.

He will place unreasonable demands upon you. He will tell you what to do, when to do it, how to do it, and when it should be completed. The king of the castle is a perfectionist. The problem is that perfection does not exist, but he will make sure that you carry the burden of making excellence a reality for him. He is very particular in the way things are to be done and will lose control if things are moved out of place.

The king of the castle will create a schedule of endless tasks that will keep you busy from the time you wake up until the time you go to sleep. He will subject you to physical violence if you fall short of his time schedule tasks or fall short carrying out perfection. He does not allow for time allowances. Just one move out of his rigid schedule can subject you to physical violence.

Knight in Shining Armor

Does your mate act as if your goals, talents, and abilities aren't good enough?
Does he tell you not to worry because he will take care of it?
Does your mate tell you how cruel the world is?
Does your mate act overprotective?
Does he tell you not to trust others?
Do you feel as if you cannot function without him?
Do you seek his approval before you do anything?
Does he act as if you cannot do anything without him?
When questioning him, does he tell you that it is too complicated for you to understand?

If you can answer yes to some of the questions above, chances are, you are with a knight in shining armor. You may find yourself seeking approval from him for everything you do because he may say that doing things on your own can land you in big trouble. He wants to rescue you from the cruel world by telling you not to worry because he will take care of everything for you. There's no need to pursue your goals, as he will rescue you so you don't have to.

The knight in shining armor will avoid answering questions that will empower you. If you seek advice from him, he will say, "Don't worry about it" or "It is too complicated for you to understand" or "I'm too busy to answer." He will minimize your intelligence, talents, and abilities and act as if your goals aren't worth pursuing.

Once he has gained your trust, the knight in shining armor may convince you not to trust your family and friends. Before you know it, you will feel too paranoid to trust anyone else but him and will isolate yourself from others. In time, you may begin to feel a sense of anxiety, fear, confusion, and lack of confidence, and you will feel distrustful of yourself and others.

With the knight in shining armor taking care of everything for you, you may feel less confident in doing things on your own and feel as if you cannot function without him. If you show signs of independence, the knight in shining armor will cause you to feel frightened by telling you more details about how cruel the world is to prevent you from becoming independent.

He, however, uses the father-figure image as a disguise to control you and to prevent you from leaving him. He will cause you to become dependent upon him and then resent your reliance. He knows you will eventually come to him for some fatherly advice. Once you seek his advice, however, he will change his position. You may hear him say, "Can't you think for yourself?" or "Why don't you grow up?"

The Competitor

Does your mate try to top you?
Does he compete with you?
Does he act as if you are his opponent?
Does he undermine your intelligence?
Does he act like he can do it better?
Does he sabotage your projects?
Does he criticize your talents and abilities?
Does he make you look like the bad guy?
Does he try to steal the attention you receive from others?

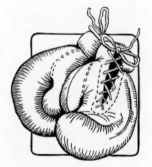

Does he buddy up with others to make you feel like an outcast?
Does he go out of his way to get others to like him better than you?

If you have answered yes to some of these questions, chances are, you are with a competitor. Instead of being a partner, he will seek a relationship in which he can compete. Those who engage in this behavior type are not on your side, for they will go out of their way to top your intelligence, talents, and abilities. He will also compete with you to win over your family, friends, and even your pets. Competition is their game, and they will treat you as an opponent instead of a partner.

If you are knowledgeable about something, you can be sure that the competitor will find a way to top you. He will read up on the very same subject just to undermine your intelligence. He unfortunately may not stop here. If you are involved in a project, he will find a way to show you that he can do it better. Some may even destroy the project you are working on. Accomplishing your goal may make you look better than him.

The competitor is good at making you look like the bad guy in the presence of others. If you tell the children that they cannot have ice cream before dinner, he will go ahead and give it to them. He will even override your authority to get the children to like him better than you by giving them the impression that you are the bad guy. He will even make up stories about something you did to him and tell others just to make you look bad.

The competitor may not only compete for the things you have or desire, but he will also try to steal the attention you are receiving from others. He will interrupt a conversation between you, your family members, and/ or friends. If you are playing with your pets, he will give them treats just to move their attention away from you. The competitor will also attempt to make you feel like an outcast. He will buddy up with others in your presence just to make you jealous.

The Ventriloquist

Does your mate tell you that you're imagining or hearing things?
Does he tell you what you are thinking or feeling?
Does he seem to recognize everyone else except you?
Does he reject your expressions?
Does he define your identity?
Does he tell you that you are crazy?
Does he deny what he says to you?
Does he act as if you are not there?
Does he accuse you of abusing or attacking him?
Does he identify you as if he does not know you?
Does he act as if you don't have a mind of your own?
Does he accuse you of doing things you're not doing?
Does he become irritated when you disagree?

If you can answer yes to some of the questions above, you may be with a ventriloquist. If you are in a relationship with a ventriloquist, his behavior may surprise you. He will take on a relationship and then act as if he does not have one. Don't be surprised if you feel alone even when you are with him. Once your relationship gets to a deeper level, he will act as if you don't exist.

There's no need to express your thoughts, feelings, or opinions to the ventriloquist because he will express them for you. He will try to take ownership of your mind as if you didn't have one. He will reject your expressions and change them to what he believes they should be. He will change your thoughts and feelings when you express them and then will tell you what you are thinking and feeling even if it isn't that.

The ventriloquist will treat you as if you were his ventriloquist doll. If you tell him that you are feeling sad, he will tell you that you are not. If you express your thoughts, he will say, "That's not what you are thinking!" He will define your whole identity as if you never had one.

The ventriloquist will have you feeling as if you are living in the twilight zone. He will alter your identity and replace it with another. He will identify you as if he never knew you. He will reject your thoughts and feelings as if you don't have the right to express them. Through the eyes of the ventriloquist, you are just a puppet, one without a mind, feelings, or needs. His goal is to take over your mind. He thinks you are just a toy without a mind that needs to be brought to life by his crawling inside of your mind to control everything that comes from it.

Conversations with the ventriloquist can be extremely confusing because he will twist your words along with his own. Not only will he alter what you say to him, he will also deny what he says to you. Interacting with him will leave you mentally confused and exhausted. He will unfortunately have your head spinning in endless confusion.

If you try to get the ventriloquist to acknowledge your thoughts and feelings, he will ignore, deny, and alter them. If you confront him about feeling neglected, he will say, "That's not how you feel," or he will tell you that you are imagining things. If you confront him about his hurtful behaviors, he will deny it and say you are abusing or attacking him.

The Victimizer

Does your mate antagonize you?
Does he provoke you to anger?
Do you feel stressed out?
Does he accuse you of abusing him?
Does your mate deny that he is abusive?
Do you feel as if you are living with a tyrant?
Does he say things that are offensive to you?
Does he deliberately invade your personal space?
Does he lock himself in another room when you confront him?
Does he try to make you feel guilty for defending yourself against his antagonistic behaviors?

Can you answer yes to some of the questions above? If you have answered yes to some of the questions, than you may be dealing with a victimizer, a perpetrator who tries to escape accountability by pretending to be the victim. The victimizer will cause extreme mental anguish by using antagonistic behaviors. He will provoke you to anger by saying something offensive, invading your personal space, or blocking you from entering or leaving a room. If you confront him about his antagonizing behaviors, he will ignore you just to get you to come after him.

Not only will the victimizer antagonize you to provoke you to anger, he will increase your anger all the more by accusing you of abusing him when you defend against his antagonistic behavior. Once you confront him about his behavior, don't be surprised if he runs into another room and locks the door, claiming he needs protection from you. The problem is you are not victimizing him in the first place. The victimizer is good at convincing himself that he is the injured party, but he isn't good at convincing you that you are the bad guy. To make matters worse, he will give others the impression that you are secretly abusing him.

Other Abusive Behaviors to Watch Out For

Mentally abusive mates are good at trying to get you to submit to their control. Unfortunately, they will also engage in other controlling behaviors to prevent you from resisting their control and leaving them. The following are some other mentally abusive behaviors to watch out for:

- **Manipulation.** Most abusers will manipulate and play with your emotions to get you to submit to their control. They will withhold affection and give you the cold shoulder to make you feel guilty and to make it appear as if you are the problem. Some will go as far as withholding resources such as money, car keys, and important information. Some will even threaten to take away the children to make it difficult for you to leave the abusive environment.

- **Sleep Deprivation.** Some abusers will deliberately interrupt your sleep to wear you down to get you to bend to their will and to prevent you from leaving them.

- **Servitude.** Some will keep you busy serving them from morning until bedtime so you do not have the energy to engage in anything else that would empower you.

- **The Apology Trap.** Some will also play with your emotions by apologizing for their behaviors to give you a false sense of hope that things will get better. Many will say, "I'm sorry," along with promises of change to get you to believe that they will change. They will also top off their words by giving you flowers to move your focus away from their behaviors.

Nonverbal Abuse

Nonverbal abuse, like the other forms of emotional abuse, can cause you to question your experiences, judgment, intuition, perception, inner trust, and sanity. Abusers carry out nonverbal abuse first through action and then other forms of emotional abuse. Recall the discussion about the movie *Gaslight* and how it demonstrates nonverbal abuse and other emotionally abusive behaviors. For example, the husband character engages in nonverbal abuse by taking a brooch out of his wife's purse without her knowledge. He then sets her up for more abuse by demeaning her and accusing her of losing it when she couldn't find it.

In order to be fully aware of the crazy-making forms of abuse, we must also be aware of nonverbal abusive behaviors because they can alter the normal function of our mind like other forms of mental abuse. Sometimes, other verbally abusive behaviors follow nonverbal abuse. For example, you go with your mate to a company-sponsored Christmas party. He doesn't introduce you to his coworkers, or he ignores you while talking to them. Or he takes you to lunch and then talks about himself or someone else but doesn't acknowledge you. Or he makes plans with you and then breaks them or plans them with someone else without telling you.

These examples demonstrate how one uses this form of abuse to cause another to feel jealous, diminished, invisible, unworthy, and left out. If you were to confront someone about these type of behaviors, he or she would come up with seemingly valid excuses that may cause you to doubt your perception of your experience and the feelings that his or her abusive behaviors provoked. Be aware of someone who does any of the following:

- doesn't acknowledge you when you are in his presence or talks only about himself or other people
- makes you feel like an outcast when in the presence of others
- undermines you in front of others
- interferes when you are interacting with another or tries to move away the attention you are receiving from others

There are other behaviors that are nonverbally abusive. These behaviors are first played out with action, following with abuse that is verbally communicated. This type of nonverbal abuse is also used to cause one to doubt her experience and sanity. Be on the lookout for the following:

- claims that things have disappeared and accusations that you have taken them or lost them without remembering
- claims of missing money and accusations that you have taken it or spent it without realizing it
- things being moved out of place and accusations that you have moved them without remembering
- personal things that are suddenly missing, especially when you know where you have placed them
- your mate saying something and then claiming he never said it, followed by accusations that you are hearing or imagining things or you are crazy
- strange occurrences that happen shortly after your mate leaves the house and accusations that you are crazy once you tell your mate about them
- consistent physical invasions of your personal space, such as a mate bumping into you, jumping out at you, throwing things in your direction in a playful manner, and other invasions of your

physical space, such as sparring or blocking you from entering or leaving a room in a playful manner and so forth

- claims it was an accident or joke or happened because of a bad dream if it occurs during sleep
- upsetting incidents and claims that these incidents never happened, followed by accusations that you are imagining them or you are crazy
- accusations that you do things you are not doing, followed by claims that you are doing them without remembering
- continuous denial of behavior and denial of the impact of his actions
- trying to move away from the topic of discussion, beginning to talk about something that is unrelated, ignoring your questions or becoming irritated when you stay on the topic
- questioning your mental state or overly showing concern for your mental health, especially when you confront him about upsetting incidents
- minimization or invalidation of your feelings when you express them or telling you what you are thinking or feeling

Stalking

Some people will unfortunately engage in two or more abusive behaviors to maintain their control over their partners. Some will indulge in the behaviors of the knight in shining armor and victimizer. Others may indulge in the behaviors of the bully and corrections officer. Some may engage in the behaviors of the prison warden and ventriloquist, but many abusive mates will engage in the behaviors of stalking once you separate from them.

The game of hide-and-seek used to be fun to play when we were children; however, it becomes dangerous when someone plays this game as an adult. Many abusers, however, play this dangerous game with women whenever they end their relationships.

Does your mate follow you? Does he show up at your doorstep? Does he accuse you of having an affair? Is he harassing you at work? Does he make threatening phone calls? Is he threatening to harm you, your family, or pets? Does he call your family and friends to try to find you? Does he sit in his car parked in front of your workplace or home?

If you are experiencing some of the above behaviors, your former mate may have turned into a stalker. Once you end your relationship, he will phone you repeatedly, promising to change his behaviors to get you to come back. If you ignore his calls, he will increase his abuse by leaving threatening voicemail messages to take away the children or to harm you and/or your extended family members and friends.

If you do not respond to his calls and are nowhere to be found, he will go out of his way and hunt you down. He will show up at your workplace and drive by other places that you have visited. He will call your extended family members and friends and even threaten them to locate you. If they ignore his calls, chances are, he will show up at their doorsteps.

Many abusive mates will turn to stalking behaviors once their relationships have ended. Many women who are stalked by their former mates are forced to go in hiding with their children just to protect themselves. Women should not have to flee their homes with their children to protect themselves from an abusive mate. Laws need to change to protect the freedom of women. Women should not have to bear the consequences and inconvenience of uprooting their children from their surroundings because of an abuser.

PART 3

Contributors to Abusive Behavior

Abusive behaviors stem from a mate's underlying insecurities and/or feelings of powerlessness. These personality traits may also stem from learned behaviors, cultural or religious beliefs, undiagnosed mental illness, or social conditioning. These contributors may possibly determine the type of behavior a mate will engage in. Most abusive men feel the desire to control their partners because it gives them a false sense of inner control. Their abusive behaviors may be provoked by:

- **Learned behaviors.** Abusers may have learned to be abusive because they may have witnessed or experienced emotional and/or physical abuse in their past. If this is the case, they will act accordingly to what they have learned and bring it into their relationships.

- **Undiagnosed mental illness.** Some may suffer from an undiagnosed mental illness because of a chemical imbalance of the brain.

- **Projection.** Abusive people tend to deny their thoughts, feelings, and actions. They will typically project their insecurities or feelings of powerlessness upon their partners. That is, they will cause their partners to experience their insecurities or feelings of powerlessness by abusing them. Abusers will eventually describe their partners as themselves.

- **Sexism.** Sexist behaviors may be passed down through male generations within the family. Peer pressure and the need to fit in with other males may also provoke sexism.

- **Religion.** Misinterpretations of religious teachings can also contribute to abusive behaviors. Many men misinterpret or abuse the Bible's teachings about the role of a husband and wife. Many husbands will abuse and treat their wives as if they owned them and may justify their abuse based on the Bible's teachings.

- **Cultural acceptance.** Some countries allow the inequality of women. We have heard about the mistreatment of women in some countries throughout the media. The 1991 movie *Not Without My Daughter* is based on the true story of an American woman who married an Iranian man. The husband took his wife to his country to meet his family but never returned to the United States. She escaped with her daughter, left his country, and returned to the United States because of the abuse that her husband subjected her to.

- **Entertainment industry.** The entertainment industry creates movies that promote violence against women. They also expose women as nothing more than sex objects. The gaming industry encourages our children to participate in the degradation of women by creating video games that depicts violence against females. Because of the exposure from the entertainment industry, our society has become desensitized when it comes to violence against women.

- **Social conditioning.** Many men continue to make derogatory jokes about women when grouping with their male counterparts.

- **Insecurities.** Abusers have feelings of low self-esteem and self-worth, along with beliefs of powerlessness, which may stem from childhood experiences. Many will unfortunately project their underlying issues upon their partners.

PART 4

Reasons Why Abusers Abuse

Abusers control their partners because they lack inner control of themselves. Most will act as if their partners externally regulate their behaviors, and they will act as if they are not responsible for them. They will blame their partners for their low feelings and hold them accountable for their behaviors. Because they are influenced by what their partners say and do, they will abuse them to regulate how they will act, believing it will give them inner control.

Deep down inside, an abusive mate feels insecure, but he will not let you know it. Most feel anger, low self-esteem, unworthiness, and powerless within. They will project their underlying issues and feelings upon their partners by causing them to experience them. They project their insecurities and feelings of powerlessness upon their partners by directing their abuse, hoping their low feelings will not return to them.

Many project their feelings and insecurities by engaging in abusive behaviors such as the bully, corrections officer, king of the castle, knight in shining armor, competitor, prison warden, victimizer, or ventriloquist, and most will engage in stalking behaviors once their relationships have ended. The specific type of behavior a mate exposes may determine his possible projection and underlying insecurities. In this section, we will go over the different personality traits that are common in abusive men and expose their underlying insecurities and projections that may cause them to indulge in specific abusive behaviors.

Bully

- *possible underlying cause*: fear of being powerless
- *possible projection*: powerlessness

If you are with the bully, chances are, his physical power intimidates you. You may also feel confused as to why he keeps picking a fight with you without cause. You may also be confused as to why he invades your personal space by blocking you from entering or leaving a room or coming up close to your face when you stand up to his bullying behavior.

Bully behaviors surround physical power. He may have a problem with his underlying feelings of powerlessness because of a past experience. He may have been subjected to humiliation in his past and placed in a powerless position. He may have recurring feelings of anger because he couldn't defend himself at the time. He may have recurring feelings of humiliation due to his experience of being powerless, which may provoke him to abuse his physical power.

To avoid his feelings of humiliation and powerlessness, the bully will project his feelings of humiliation and powerlessness upon you, his partner. He will abuse his physical power by placing you in a powerless position to cause you to experience his feelings of humiliation and powerlessness. He may have learned from his past experiences that, in order to feel powerful, he must take away others' power.

The bully may be angry because he lacked the physical power to prevent the humiliation he suffered in his past. He may exercise his physical power to make sure that he never encounters the humiliation and powerlessness he once experienced. He may occasionally challenge your physical power to challenge his powerfulness. He will avoid those of equal power, and to maintain his power, he will only target those who are smaller than he is.

Corrections Officer

- *possible underlying cause*: low self-worth
- *possible projection*: not good enough

The corrections officer will constantly be on the lookout for your flaws and make negative comments about your physical appearance and actions as if they need to be fixed. His behavior surrounds his feelings of low self-worth. Chances are, he was constantly criticized in his past to the point where he feels worthless. He may have been brought up in a strict environment where his worthiness was based on perfection and performance. As a result, he projects his feelings of not being good enough upon you, his partner.

The corrections officer projects his unworthiness by pointing out your imperfections, and he will criticize your talents, abilities, and performances to cause you to feel as if you are not good enough. He will lower your self-worth because it turns his feelings of unworthiness into worthiness. Because his projection surrounds his low self-worth, he may only value you based on perfection or performance. The problem is that perfection does not exist. And because it does not, you may never be good enough for him.

Prison Warden

- *possible underlying causes*: abandonment, separation anxiety
- *possible projection*: unworthiness

The prison warden's behavior surrounds his underlying feelings of unworthiness and his fear of abandonment and separation anxiety. Chances are, he may have been neglected or abandoned in his past and suffered from separation anxiety, which may have provoked his feelings of unworthiness.

Because the prison warden focuses on his feelings of unworthiness and his abandonment and separation anxiety, he in turn will project his feelings of unworthiness by subjecting you to abuse to cause you to experience his feelings, which will cause you to become distant. Because he blocks his abusive behavior from himself, the prison warden may not associate his abusive behavior as the cause of your distance. He will assume that your distance is caused by an outside affair rather than his abusive behavior and will act according to his suspicion. Because of his denial, he may begin accusing you of having an affair to justify your distance.

Once you try to end the relationship, the prison warden may increase his abuse because of his fear of abandonment, which will provoke his feelings of separation anxiety. He may threaten or use physical violence to prevent you from leaving to prevent his fear of abandonment and his feelings of separation anxiety. He unfortunately victimizes himself by causing his own abandonment and feelings of separation anxiety by directing his abusive behavior. It's a no-win situation for you and him.

King of the Castle

- *possible underlying causes*: religion, sexism, social acceptance, learned behaviors
- *possible projection*: subordination

The king of the castle's behavior surrounds sexism. He may have learned to suppress his feelings because he may have been taught that expression of feeling is feminine. He may have an underlying fear of being viewed as weak, so he goes to the opposite extreme by suppressing his feelings instead of expressing them.

The king of the castle will avoid stepping into the feminine side at all costs. Do not ask him to help you clean the dishes or help you with the children, even if you work outside of the home, because it would be a detriment to his masculinity. His attitude appears to be "anti-female." He is rough around the edges and comes off "too tough" with women. He is not the romantic type because romance requires the expression of feelings, which he associates as feminine.

The king of the castle will withhold equality in his relationship because of his sexist beliefs. He will make all of the decisions and prevent you from having a say. Expect him to watch the sports channel and nothing else. He views women as weak; therefore, he will treat you as if you were a subordinate there just to serve and benefit him.

Knight in Shining Armor

- *possible underlying causes*: low self-esteem, fear of abandonment
- *possible projection*: inferiority complex

The knight in shining armor acts as a father figure who wants to protect you from the cruel world by doing everything for you. Once he tells you how cruel the world is, you may not even want to pursue your goals. You may not want to do anything without him. After all, the world is a scary place.

The behavior of the knight in shining armor may surround an underlying inferiority complex problem. Chances are, the knight in shining armor may have been subjected to an inferior position in his past. Someone may have prevented him from becoming independent so he or should could maintain control over him.

The knight in shining armor may have been treated as if he were not competent to handle things on his own, which may have contributed to his inferiority complex problem. He projects his inferior complex problem by causing you to experience his feelings of inadequacy. He will cause you to feel inferior by using emotional abuse to lower your self-worth, which will boost his self-esteem.

The knight in shining armor will use guilt and fear to cause you to feel incompetent and afraid to do things on your own. He boosts his confidence by lowering yours. An underlying fear of abandonment may also cause his behavior. By placing you in a dependent state of mind, chances are, you will be too afraid to leave him.

Competitor

- *possible underlying cause*: low self-worth
- *possible projections*: jealousy, unworthiness, and feelings of inadequacy

The competitor's behavior surrounds his feelings of low self-worth. Chances are, he may have been compared to others in his past. He may have been valued based on performance and may have been told that he doesn't measure up. Being compared to others may have provoked his strong desire to compete.

The competitor will project his feelings of unworthiness by minimizing or negating your talents and abilities. He projects his feelings of inadequacy by topping you. He will compete to make him look better than you are. He will challenge your intelligence and even sabotage or destroy a project you are working on just so he doesn't feel as if he doesn't measure up.

Not only does the competitor project his feelings of inadequacy, he also displays his jealous frame of mind. He may have been neglected in his past because he didn't measure up, which may have contributed to his feelings of jealousy. He projects his feelings of jealousy by stealing the attention you receive from others. He will buddy up with others in your presence to make you feel like an outcast.

The competitor will unfortunately not view you as his partner and treat you only as his opponent. He is not a team player and will do anything to be at the top, even if it is at your expense. Unfortunately, he has a problem with sharing the spotlight. He is so greedy for attention that he will make you struggle to hold on to the attention you are receiving from your family or friends while in his presence.

Ventriloquist

- *possible underlying cause*: problem with separateness
- *possible projection*: identity, denial

Once the ventriloquist gets deeply involved in his relationship, he will no longer see beyond himself and recognize your identity. He will treat you as if you have no mind, spirit, thoughts, feelings, or needs. He will re-create your identity and treat you as if you were a ventriloquist doll.

If you are feeling invisible with the ventriloquist, chances are, he has shifted his identity, so he will no longer recognize yours. He will still act out his identity, but he will mentally deny that it's his own. Because he mentally shifted his identity, where did it go? He unfortunately shifted his identity upon you.

The ventriloquist will overshadow your identity, like an eclipse of the sun and moon, so you and he become enmeshed as one, him. Once he does this, he will identify his self through you and act as if his identity were yours instead of his own. The ventriloquist, however, will still act out his identity but will deny it's his own. He has a problem with his identity because he rejects it. He seems to be confused when it comes to identifying his own identity and seems to be confused about recognizing yours.

Because he shifted his identity, the ventriloquist will eventually describe you as himself and accuse you for any wrongdoings his identity commits. He convinces himself that he isn't responsible for what he is acting out. He recognizes his true identity, but unfortunately, he only recognizes it as if it were yours. Because of his denial, he will direct his abusive behavior and deny he is abusive. He will refute the pain he inflicts. When it comes to an intimate relationship with the ventriloquist, there is no room for two.

Someone in his past may have invalidated the ventriloquist's feelings, experiences, and existence. Chances are, the ventriloquist has been treated as if he didn't exist. Because of his past experiences, he may have projected his identity along with the feelings and experiences that came with it because he may have been taught that all those were not valid.

Because his feelings and experiences were denied, he will act as if his identity doesn't exist. Not only does he reject his own self, he will project his repudiation by denying your identity as well. Through the mind of the ventriloquist, he doesn't exist, and because he doesn't, then neither do you. If his experiences never occurred, than neither did yours. If his feelings are not valid, neither are yours. All of the bad experiences, feelings, and events that took place in his life were real, but someone in his past invalidated them. What the ventriloquist needs to acknowledge is that his identity is separate from your own.

Victimizer

- *possible underlying causes*: abuse, neglect, lack of discipline, or rebellious disorder
- *possible projections*: victimization, perpetrator, or denial

The victimizer acts like a child in need of discipline. He will antagonize and frustrate you enough to get you to come after him. He will act out the perpetrator role by subjecting you to mental anguish and then play the victim role once you react to his antagonizing behaviors.

The victimizer's behaviors surround his past victimization. The problem is that he is no longer the victim because he acts as a perpetrator. He unfortunately projects the behaviors of his perpetrator and projects his victimization. Chances are, he has been victimized in his past and then became a perpetrator to "settle the score" with the perpetrator from his past. But you are not the perpetrator. The victimizer may also have been neglected in his past because he will go out of his way to get attention. He may have acted out negative behaviors in his past in order to get attention, or he may have an undiagnosed mental disorder that may have prevented him from being cooperative.

Stalker

- *possible underlying causes*: fear of abandonment, rejection
- *possible projections*: denial, victimization

Once you have separated from an emotional abuser, he may begin to engage in stalking behaviors. He will do anything to prevent you from leaving even when he is subjecting you to abuse. If you are nowhere to be found, he will go out of his way to hunt you down.

Many mates are in denial of their abusive behaviors, and they will project their rejection by denying the pain they cause their partners. Many abusive mates engage in stalking behaviors because of their underlying fear of abandonment and rejection. They will unfortunately make this their reality. They will drive you away with their abusive behaviors and accusations, which are based on their fear of rejection and abandonment, not facts. Unfortunately, they will blame you for rejecting and abandoning them instead of blaming their abusive behaviors.

Because they are so focused on their fear of abandonment and rejection, they will bring about their own isolation because of their abusive behaviors and denial. Many have witnessed or encountered abuse in their pasts. Unfortunately, many still see themselves as victims even when they are subjecting someone else to their abusive behaviors.

PART 5

Confronting Abusive Behaviors

If you are in an abusive relationship, chances are, you are feeling frustrated, confused, stressed out, depressed, and exhausted. You may know that something is wrong in your relationship but cannot seem to find the problem. You are probably thinking that it isn't abuse because he hasn't hit you yet. Because you cannot find the problem, you continue walking on eggshells, thinking of ways not to upset him.

You may be trying to figure out why he is angry, so you ask him, only to get an answer of "I'm not angry." You may have tried to find peace by talking to him, only to have him deny his abusive behaviors and accuse you of attacking him. Dealing with abusive behaviors isn't easy. An abusive mate can frustrate you. You will feel stressed out, alone, angry, ignored, depressed, and extremely confused. In this section, we will go over the reaction you may get if you confront a mentally abusive mate about his behaviors.

If you are dealing with an abusive mate, you need to consider certain things before you decide to confront him about his behaviors. Most abusers deny their abusive behaviors. Confronting an abusive mate about his behaviors may place you at risk for physical harm. Because abusive mates deny their behaviors, your abusive mate may view your confrontation as an attack rather than a defense.

Many abusive mates are dealing with past issues, and they will not react to a confrontation in a rational manner. Many are unconsciously acting out their past experiences and not living in the present moment. They are stuck in the past, trying to settle the score to eliminate their pain. They may be unconsciously reenacting their past to seek vengeance against their perpetrators. Unfortunately, many are not aware that they are taking out their vengeance on their partners.

Because of their denial, your abusive mate may not be aware that he causes your distress. He can, however, see your reaction and will react defensively to your reaction, as if he were being victimized. In this section, I will give you a rundown on the potential risks that you may encounter with each abusive personality type and the way they may react if you confront them about their behaviors.

- **Bully.** The bully has a problem with his feelings of powerlessness. Because he exercises his physical power to avoid feeling powerless, you may be at risk for physical violence if you confront him about his abusive behavior. Because the bully denies his abusive behavior, he may view your confrontation as a threat to his physical power. So he may resort to physical violence to maintain his powerful stance.

- **Corrections Officer.** The corrections officer has a perfectionist view of himself. To boost his perfect image, he will criticize and find fault in everyone around him. And that includes you. Because he is emotionally abusive, he may also deny his abusive behavior. Should you confront him about his abusive behavior, he may view your confrontation as an attack on his perfect image, so he may subject you to physical violence to prevent you from breaking down the perfectionist view he has of himself.

- **Prison Warden.** The prison warden has a problem with rejection and abandonment. Because he is abusive, he may deny his abusive behavior. The prison warden tends to use physical violence to maintain control over his partner. Because he denies his abusive behavior, he may view your confrontation as a threat to reject and abandon him, so he may use physical violence to prevent you from leaving and to prevent his feelings of abandonment and separation anxiety from reaching his consciousness.

- **King of the Castle.** The king of the castle may feel privileged because he is a man. He will not show equality when it comes to women. He overly exaggerates his masculinity to the point of acting as if he is anti-female. Because he feels privileged, he may view your confrontation as a challenge to his masculinity, so he may feel privileged to use his physical power to keep you in a subordinate and controlled position.

- **Knight in Shining Armor.** The knight in shining armor has an inferiority complex problem and feelings of unworthiness. He is emotionally abusive but exposes his abuse in deceptive ways and will project his lowliness. He denies his abusive behavior, so he may view your confrontation as a challenge to his superiority. So he may use physical violence to put you back in the inferior position to maintain his feelings of supremacy.

- **Competitor.** The competitor has a problem with low self-worth and jealousy. He is not on your side because he acts as if you were his opponent. He has an "I win when you lose" attitude and will do anything to make sure he comes out on top. He loves challenges because he will test you when there is no contest. Because he denies his abusive behavior, he may view your confrontation as a threat of losing and may subject you to physical violence to make sure he wins.

- **Ventriloquist.** The ventriloquist will treat you as if you were a doll. He is emotionally abusive and denies his identity and yours. When it comes to the ventriloquist, there is no room for two. If he denies his own identity and yours, chances are, he will repudiate his abusive behavior. He has a problem with his identity, and he will only view you as an extension of him. By shifting his identity over to you, he will not acknowledge you as a separate person. If you confront him about his behavior, he may view your confrontation as a separation from his enmeshment, so he may subject you to physical violence to make sure that he remains the only one.

- **Victimizer.** The victimizer has a problem with his conduct. He will antagonize you and try to escape accountability by trying to convince you that he is the victim. He may have been victimized in his past, but he is the perpetrator at the present. He projects his victimization even though he is the perpetrator. Because of his denial, he may view your confrontation as victimization and resort to physical violence to turn him back into the perpetrator.

Stalking

Stalking behaviors represent the end-stage of an abuser's relationship. He may apologize and promise to change his behavior. He will even go to counseling to prevent you from leaving. He will overly indulge you with flowers and gifts to convince you that he is changing for the better. Should you buy into his promises of change and decide to stay in the relationship, he may start the abusive cycle all over again. He believes he needs to regulate you in order to maintain inner control of himself. If you do not accept his empty promises of change and are ready to end the relationship, he may increase his abuse and engage in stalking behaviors. To regain control, he will increase his abuse and become extremely dangerous.

Because most abusers deny their abusive behaviors, many will not react in a rational manner when you confront them about their actions. Because of this, I do not recommend that you confront an abuser about his behavior because of the risk of physical violence. Unfortunately, you cannot control your mate's behavior, but you can control what you will tolerate. If you decide that you want to end an abusive relationship, do not tell your mate that you plan to leave. Seek outside help so you can get out safely. The next section will explore ways to protect yourself.

PART 6

Protecting Yourself

Confronting an abusive mate about his behaviors can put you at risk for harm. If you or anyone you know is experiencing abusive behaviors, please seek help with a counselor who is trained in controlling behaviors. Or call the National Domestic Violence Hotline at (800) 799-SAFE, which has more information.

Once your abusive mate senses that you want to end the relationship, he may increase his abuse to prevent you from leaving. He may begin making threats, resorting to physical violence, and/or taking away important resources such as money, car keys, as well as important documents such as bank statements, bills and tax information, and immunization and health records to prevent you from leaving. If you find yourself in an abusive relationship, you can take steps to protect yourself. If possible, take these steps at the first sign of abusive behaviors and before an abuser senses that you are ending the relationship.

1. **Seek outside help.** Please seek outside help with a counselor who is trained in controlling behaviors, or call the Domestic Violence Hotline for information and support. You may also want to contact an attorney to find out what your options are. Check the blue pages in your phone book for a list of attorneys. If your funds are limited, contact the Legal Aid office in your area.

2. **Gather all important documents.** Gather and copy all important documents and keep them in a file box that you do not keep in the house. Leave it with a trusted relative or friend. If no one is available, place the following documents in a safe

deposit box: bank account statements, tax papers, mortgage loan information, credit card accounts, Social Security information, birth certificates, passports, health records, such as immunization records, personal phone/address book, copies of all bills, such as phone, electric and gas bills, and so forth.

3. **Copy.** Get copies of house and car keys, along with any other keys not mentioned, and keep all in the file box.

4. **Open a separate bank account.** Many abusive husbands will drain all joint bank accounts and leave you high and dry once they sense that you are ending the relationship. I recommend that you open a separate bank account in your name only, have the bank statements sent to a different address, and put money into this account periodically.

5. **Open a post office (PO) box account.** Sometimes an abusive mate will go through your mail or withhold it from you. You can have your mail delivered to a PO box located at the post office to prevent your mate from accessing your mail. You can also have your bank statements sent to your PO box if you cannot have them delivered to another address.

6. **Open a safe deposit box.** If you cannot leave any documents at a relative's or friend's house for some reason, you can open a safe deposit box at your bank and keep important documents there. You can open a safe deposit box account for about fifty to sixty dollars a year.

7. **Create a journal of any abusive episodes that occur between you and your mate.** Write down the date, the details of what happened, and the location of where they took place. Keep this dated journal in your purse, or hide it where your mate cannot find it. A dated journal can be used as evidence should you need to go to court at a later time.

8. **Protect yourself from threats and/or physical violence.** If your mate verbally threatens or physically abuses you, you may be able to get a restraining/protection order that the court issues. It may remove your abuser from the house and prevent him from contacting you or coming near you. The typical time frame of a protection order is anywhere from six months up to a year. If he violates the order, he can be arrested. When you apply for a restraining/protection order and it is granted, you must also obey this order because it applies to both you and your abusive mate. You must also obey this order to prevent contact by not contacting your mate by phone or any other means. You must stay away from him during the time the order is active.

PART 7

Dealing with Stalking Behaviors

According to the statistics from the National Coalition against Domestic Violence, one in twelve women has been stalked in her lifetime. Specifically, 81 percent of women who were stalked by a current or former intimate partner were also physically abused by the same partner.[5]

What Is Stalking?

Stalking consists of unwanted attention that is directed at one by another. According to the stalking fact sheet from the National Center for Victims of Crime, three in four victims are stalked by someone they know.[6] Stalking typically occurs when a partner has separated from an abusive mate. According to the stalking handbook for victims, from the National Center for Victims of Crime, typical behavior patterns of stalkers include.[7]

- **Having unwanted contact, the most common behavior patterns of stalkers.** Stalkers will gather information about their victims first. Then they will follow, send letters and unwanted e-mails, leave notes, and send and make repeated phone calls to their victims.

---

5   Source: www.ncadv.org/files/DomesticViolenceFactSheet(National).pdf (May 2013).
6   Source: www.victimsofcrime.org/docs/src/stalking-fact-sheet_english. pdf?sfvrsn=4 (August 2013).
7   Source: http://www.victimsofcrime.org/docs/src/stalking-a-handbook-for-victims.pdf?sfvrsn=2 (pg. 17) (August 2013).

- **Sending flowers and gifts.** Many stalkers will go out of their way and send flowers and gifts to their victims, hoping to get a loving reaction from them in return. If the stalker does not get the desired reaction from his victim, however, things can get worse.

- **Following.** If the stalker does not get a reaction from his victim from communicating through letters, e-mails, or phone calls, he may begin to physically appear. Stalkers are typically obsessed with their victims and may follow them wherever they go or show up where they happen to be. Some stalkers will park in front of victims' houses or at their workplace for hours, just to get attention from their victims. If the victim continues to reject and avoid the stalker, his stalking behaviors may increase to a more dangerous level.

- **Increasing stalking behaviors to dangerous levels.** Some stalkers will end their stalking activities at some point in time. Some stalkers, however, will take their behaviors to more dangerous levels. If the victim continues to avoid the stalker, he may make repeated calls and then hang up or leave threatening messages on the answering machine. He may also leave threatening letters or dead flowers or animals on the victim's property. Some stalkers will also destroy the victim's property or vehicle just because the victim rejected them.

Common Personality Traits of Stalkers

Many stalkers have low self-esteem and tend to depend on others for their happiness, so they become obsessive about pursuing their victims. Stalkers have certain personality traits that set them apart from others.[8]

- **Loners.** They are not comfortable with social gatherings and will typically avoid them. They will isolate themselves from others and expect you to do the same.

---

8   Source: http://www.victimsofcrime.org/docs/src/stalking-a-handbook-for-victims.pdf?sfvrsn=2.

- **Jealousy.** They will become jealous and accuse you of having affairs if you talk to others.
- **Possessive.** They are very possessive because of their jealousy and will act as if they own you.
- **Obsessive.** They believe you will complete them. They will forsake everything else in their lives because they believe you are responsible for their happiness.
- **Controlling.** They will control you to prevent you from leaving because they fear rejection and abandonment.
- **Quick-tempered.** They like to get their way and may quickly lose their temper if things don't go their way.
- **Cunning.** They like to get what they want and will manipulate others in clever ways to obtain what they want.
- **Deceptive.** They will claim that they care about you when all they really want is having you around to be responsible for their happiness.
- **Problem with rejection.** They have a hard time accepting rejection and will typically seek vengeance against you if you reject or abandon them.
- **Persistent.** Most will not accept no for an answer because they have difficulty accepting rejection and abandonment.
- **Irresponsible.** They will hold you accountable for their unhappiness because most believe they are not responsible for their feelings.
- **Blame others for actions.** They will blame you for their actions because they feel as if they are not responsible for their actions.
- **Self-centered.** They tend to care only about themselves and will lack empathy and concern for your well-being.
- **Feel privileged.** Most feel privileged and will act as if it is their right to hold you accountable for their feelings, behaviors, actions, and happiness.
- **Overly intelligent.** They tend to be extremely intelligent and know how to manipulate the system and others to access information.
- **Quickly falls in love.** They will fall in love rather quickly and may press you into a quick marriage or pregnancy. Or they will try to get you to move in with them so you can make them happy.

If you have recently ended an abusive relationship, your former mate may turn to stalking behaviors to get you to come back so he can maintain control over you. He will threaten and follow you, and he will even try to break into your home. He will also harass your family members and your friends. An abuser will engage in stalking behaviors to seek vengeance against you because you have rejected him and you are no longer under his control.

Stalking, however, does not only occur in intimate relationships, but it can also occur unexpectedly as well. Fortunately, I survived my encounter with a stalker, but unfortunately, many others have not. I have learned from my experiences and learned how to be creative when it came to dealing with my stalker. I will share what I have done to try to keep myself safe and some safety tips that I have learned from the officers who helped me through my ordeal.

- **Install an alarm system.** An alarm system will cost you around thirty dollars per month. If you cannot afford the monthly fees, you can get a window alarm kit from a hardware store. I had an alarm system put in my house because the stalker tried to break in twice. I didn't have enough money to protect every window in my home, so I went to the hardware store and purchased a window alarm kit that included about four mini window alarms. I installed these alarms on the windows that were not protected.

- **Use soda cans.** Fill empty soda cans with pennies, and place them on the windowsills throughout your home. Should the stalker try to come in through a window, the noise from the falling cans of pennies will alert you in time to call the police.

- **Install different types of locks.** Place various locks on doors to make it more difficult for the stalker to break in. Also, make sure that you place a lock on your bedroom door and place a jimmy up against the door. Should the stalker break into your house, you may be able to climb out of a first-floor bedroom window to seek help. I installed four different types of locks on my family-room door where my stalker tried to break in.

- **Consider getting an emergency ladder.** Use these emergency ladders to climb out of a second-story window should the stalker break in. These ladders are placed over the windowsill so you can easily climb out of the window from the second floor. You can purchase these ladders at major hardware stores. These ladders, if long enough, can help you get to the ground safely to get help. Keep this ladder in your bedroom.

- **Keep interior lights on.** Keep some interior lights on overnight, especially by entrances. I would keep my living-room lights on overnight and set the timer to have them shut off by dawn.

- **Install exterior lights.** Keep the outside of your house bright. Install exterior lights around the outside of your house, especially if you lack outside lighting. Keep outdoor lights on overnight, and use a timer or manually turn them off in the morning. Stalkers do not like to be seen, and your neighbors can keep an eye on your house and call the police if they see someone suspicious lurking around your house.

- **Clear all things outside.** Remove ladders and outdoor furniture from the patio or yard to deter the stalker from climbing up to the second-floor windows. Trim trees and bushes to deter the stalker from hiding behind them.

- **Park your car in the garage.** If you do not have a garage, consider getting a car alarm installed, and park your car in a well-lit area. Have keys ready, and check your surroundings before you get in or out of your car.

- **Install a surveillance camera.** Aim the camera eye where the activity takes place. Get extra camera eyes if you need to cover other areas. Set up your surveillance camera, and hook it up to a recorder, if possible. Record overnight, and then view the recording the next day for any activity. I set up a surveillance camera to view the stalker's activity by the front door. I covered the camera eye with black electrical tape to conceal the white color. I hooked up a video recorder to the surveillance camera and then set the timer to record overnight. I would view the tape the next morning, hoping to get his identity recorded so I could have him arrested.

- **Tell your neighbors.** The police told me to tell my neighbors about my situation, and I was glad I did. My neighbor called me one night and told me that a suspicious vehicle was parked in front of my house. I then called the police. The officers told me that telling others about my situation would keep me safer. Your neighbors will watch over you and report any suspicious activity around your house. Give your neighbors a clue that you are in trouble. For example, turn lights on and off repeatedly so they can alert the police. If you are close friends with your neighbor or have a friend who lives nearby, consider getting a two-way radio and give him or her one unit while you keep the other unit with you. If there is any sign of trouble, you can alert him or her to call the police. Some of these units have a ten-mile radius or more and do not cost much.

- **Slide down a wall to call.** If your stalker is harassing you and then suddenly disappears when the police arrive, he can possibly see you calling the police. Should you need to phone the police, stand against a wall, away from the window, and slide down into a sitting position. And then phone the police. Placing your calls to the police in this manner may help the police catch the stalker in action.

- **Keep a journal of all stalking incidents.** Make sure that you write down the date and time of all stalking incidents that have occurred. Be sure to keep this journal in your purse. This journal can help you build a case against your stalker and can be used for evidence.

- **Report all incidents.** Call the police, no matter how minor the incidents may be. Stalking is a serious problem that can put you at risk for harm. The police written reports, along with your journal of the stalking incidents, may be enough to press charges against your stalker if the police catch him.

- **Change your route.** To lessen your chances of being followed, change your route when you are driving about. Stalkers like predictability. If you are shopping for groceries, go to different stores on different days and different times to avoid being predictable. Stay in areas where there are many people. Drive on major roads, and avoid dark, isolated back roads. If you must drive at night, stay on major, well-lit roads.

- **Keep your cell phone with you at all times.** Always keep your cell phone with you and fully charged. Make sure that you have two cell phone chargers, one for your home and one to keep in your vehicle. Keep your cell phone in the bedroom with you, and do not turn it off.

- **Try not to go out alone.** Stalkers like to target their victims when they are alone. If you must travel alone, be aware of your surroundings as you get in or out of your car. Lock your car doors once you get in, and lock them after you get out. Stay in populated areas, and avoid isolated back roads. Run your errands during the day if possible.

- **Take self-defense classes.** Seek out places in your community that offer self-defense classes. If you do not have the time, you may want to consider ordering a course online. I purchased a self-defense course online that focused on pressure points. If you learn how to use the pressure points of the body to defend yourself, you can put down your stalker without much physical effort should you be attacked.

- **Consider getting a dog.** The sound of a barking dog can alert you to call the police before your stalker has a chance to break in. When taking the dog out to do his business, do not leave your dog unattended, and avoid walking the dog in dark areas. Consider walking your dog in the front yard where neighbors can see.

- **Let others know of your whereabouts.** Let family and friends know where you are at all times. Should problems arise, your family and friends will be able to track where you have been and know the last place you were when you last contacted them.

PART 8

Healing from Abuse

Unfortunately, being in an abusive relationship can take a toll on your physical and emotional health. In order to move on, you will need time to heal your wounds. I devote this section to healing your mind, body, and spirit and getting reacquainted with yourself so you can move past the abuse. The effects of abuse are painfully plentiful. If you can acknowledge that you are not the cause of your mate's abusive behavior and that you deserve better, you will be on your way to healing. The following are some insights about abuse to help move you toward recovery.

- Your mate is abusive because he has a problem with control, not you.
- An abusive mate will blame you for his unhappiness and abusiveness. If he isn't happy, he will surely take away your happiness.
- Your abusive mate will control you because he lacks inner control of himself.
- A controlling mate will cause you to experience the feelings he feels within himself.
- An abusive mate will accuse you of doing things that you are not doing and eventually fault you for what he is acting out.
- An abusive mate will reject and redefine you.
- Some may not accept you as being a separate person from themselves, and they will eventually describe you as if you were them.
- A controlling mate will tell lies about you and himself.
- You cannot do anything to change your mate's oppressive behaviors, but you can control what you will tolerate.

- A controlling mate will lower your self-esteem, self-worth, and confidence and take away your freedom to choose.
- A controlling mate will also condition you to believe that no one else will love you any more than he does.

Healing Your Mind

Encountering an emotionally abusive mate will make you feel mentally off balance to the point where nothing he says or does makes any sense. He will have you walking around in a daze, feeling disconnected from yourself and reality. He will cause you to doubt your perceptions, feelings, experiences, intuition, and inner trust and may trigger you to doubt your own sanity. He will also lower your self-esteem and cause you to feel invalidated, unworthy, diminished, less confident, depressed, lonely, inferior, and invisible. You may even blame yourself for the abuse because it was directed upon you and he will tell you that you cause his behaviors.

When you are involved in an abusive relationship for long periods of time, your mate's oppressive behaviors may unknowingly brainwash you. An oppressive mate will use emotional abuse, threats, isolation, constant supervision, financial dependency, invalidation, and emotional confusion to brainwash you into thinking that you are not worthy of anything better.

In order to heal your mind, you need to bring it back to its normal function. To boost your self-esteem and feelings of low self-worth, you need to focus on yourself and reestablish connection with your identity. And once you get connected with yourself, you can focus on regaining your inner strength and washing away the brainwashing effects. It will take some time for you to heal from the abuse, but you can begin your journey by recognizing the damage and doing what it takes to reverse it.

Undoing the Confusion

In order to heal your mind, you need to end your confusion. To do so, you need to understand your experience. I recommend that you go to domestic violence counseling sessions to learn more about emotionally abusive behaviors. Once there, you will meet other women with similar experiences. If you cannot go to the counseling sessions, read some books about emotional abuse, which I will recommend after the closing. Once you recognize the emotionally abusive behaviors that have caused your emotional distress, your confusion will eventually subside. You will feel more alert and feel more connected to yourself and your reality.

Getting Reconnected with Yourself

Being in an abusive relationship can cause you to lose sight of the person you are. You can lose touch with your identity from long-term isolation and abuse. When you are isolated from others, you have no validation of your worth, except for how he treats you and what he tells you. If he isolates you from others and constantly defines your worth, you will come to believe that you are unworthy because you have lost connection to yourself.

Your abusive mate has brainwashed you into thinking you are not worthy and has caused you to doubt your perceptions, experiences, worth, and truth of your reality so he can maintain his control over you. Once you understand what you are experiencing, you need to reconnect with your identity so you can rebuild your self-esteem to get back the power you have lost.

You may avoid focusing on yourself because you have been brainwashed into thinking that you are a lowly person. Turning the focus on yourself may cause you to feel nervous at first because you may feel as if you are reconnecting with someone you haven't seen in a long time, and that someone is you! You need to focus on yourself to rebuild your low self-esteem. The following are some tips to help you reverse the damage.

Undoing Self-Doubt

An abusive mate will brainwash you by negating your perceptions, experiences, intelligence, opinions, feelings, talents, skills, and existence to cause you to doubt yourself. Experiencing negation regularly can cause you to doubt your worth. Doubting yourself is damaging to your self-esteem. When you doubt yourself, feelings, experiences, talents, and abilities, you will lower your worth and lose the trust you had for yourself. Once you lose your inner trust, your feelings of inadequacy will paralyze you. This will cause you to rely on your abusive mate for validation, which will turn into more nullification!

Doubting yourself will rob you of your confidence and independence. It will prevent you from making decisions and doing things that are necessary to improve your life. When you doubt yourself, you give more power to your abusive mate who will cause you to feel unworthy to prevent you from moving on so he can maintain his control over you. He will take away the positive feedback that you deserve. The following tips will help you remove your self-doubt:

- Get reconnected to your identity. Once you do so, you will know who you are and what you are capable of. Then your self-doubting behavior will disappear.

- Look for the truth. Do not believe everything your mate tells you. Confirm the truth by looking at the facts, which can be discerned by looking at his actions. He can hide the truth by his words, but he cannot hide it with his actions. Actions speak louder than words!

- Believe in yourself instead of your mate. Once you connect with yourself and regain your inner trust, you will learn to believe in yourself.

- Erase his false negation of you from your mind. Don't accept his low perception of you; think of your positive qualities instead.

- Do not isolate yourself to the point where you are only with your abusive mate. Surround yourself with others so you can get the positive feedback you deserve.

Redefining Your Worth

Are you or your mate defining your worth? An abusive mate will define your worth and try to convince you to define your worth as he does. He will negate everything about you so you feel the low self-worth he feels within himself. Don't fall into his game of trying to convince him that you are worthy because he will only invalidate your value. You do not need him to feel worthy. You will find your value once you reconnect with yourself. Do not allow anyone, including your mate, to define your worth. The following statements will help you see your worth:

- You are worthy of respect because you give it.
- You are worthy of trust because you are trustworthy.
- You are worthy of compassion because you give it.
- You are worthy of consideration because you give it.
- You are worthy of love because you give it.

Undoing Self-Blame

Because your mate directs his abusive behavior upon you, you may believe that you are to blame for his oppressive behavior. You may also take on the guilt because your mate told you that you are at fault for his abusive behaviors. You may also feel guilty because you couldn't stop the abuse.

We all are responsible for our behaviors, but an abusive mate will act as if he has no control over himself because he will blame others for his abusive behaviors. Your abusive mate lacks inner control and will act as if what you say and do controls his behaviors. He will try to regulate you so he feels in control of himself. You are not to blame for your mate's behavior. You cannot make him hit you, call you derogatory names, break your things, and so forth. These actions come from him, not you. Just because he directs his abusive behaviors upon you, that doesn't mean that you are responsible for them.

Being around an oppressive mate can also cause you to subjugate yourself. You may internalize the anger because of the feelings of low self-worth, or you may engage in alcohol and/or drugs to cope with the pain. Engaging in substances will only add more problems to your existing issue. Your mate's abusive behaviors have nothing to do with you in the first place. Don't punish yourself for something you did not do!

Lowering Your Tolerance

If you stay in an abusive relationship, you will eventually adapt and increase your tolerance to the abuse, which will cause you to feel as if it were a normal occurrence. Abuse is not a normal occurrence and needs to be addressed immediately. It is not acceptable in any relationship; nor is it a way of life. You deserve better. Having a high tolerance to abuse will damage your self-esteem. To lower your tolerance, you must set boundaries for yourself of what you will and will not tolerate. Set boundaries, and do not allow anyone to cross them, including your mate.

Healing Your Body

Your body is the temple of your spirit. Your spirit will alert you to a problem by causing you to experience a physical sensation, a message from your spirit that something is wrong. If you encounter too much stress, your spirit will alert you by causing you to experience the physical sensations of a tension headache, tense muscles, and so forth. Pay attention to the physical sensations of your body. Identify if something outside of the body, such as stress, or something within the body causes the physical sensations that you are experiencing. Once you identify the problem, address it so your body can be at ease.

Healing Your Spirit

When you express your feelings to someone and he validates them, your feelings will be released from your body. Expressing your feelings to someone, only to have them invalidated, will cause your feelings to become trapped inside of you. Having an abusive mate consistently invalidating you can cause you to hold back your feelings and make you feel as if you do not matter, which is damaging to your spirit.

Because your mate consistently invalidated your feelings, you may continue to hold back your feelings long after your relationship has ended. You may restrain your emotions from your family members and friends, believing they will be invalidated if you express them. Validation, however, is important to your spiritual health. It confirms your existence and the truth of your reality and helps you release your feelings from your body.

Share your feelings with someone you trust and someone who is compassionate and willing to listen, such as a counselor who is familiar with domestic violence, a family member, or close friend. Once your feelings and past experiences are validated, they will eventually become more distant from your memory.

Acknowledging Your Feelings

Unfortunately, you may want to avoid focusing on your feelings because of the way the abuse has affected you. You may be feeling unworthy, diminished, less confident, insecure, hopeless, and depressed. You are encountering these states because of the abuse and because your mate has projected his painful feelings upon you. In other words, he has caused you to experience his inner pain by subjecting you to his abusive behavior.

It's important for you to acknowledge your feelings. They are important because they are connected to your spirit. Your feelings can guide and protect you if you acknowledge and pay attention to them. One way you can acknowledge your feelings is to write them down in a journal, which can help you release them from your body. Allow yourself to feel these feelings even if they are uncomfortable. If you avoid acknowledging them because they are painful, they will remain within, and you will continue to feel them until you deal with them. You need to release your feelings so they do not resurface again in the future.

Releasing Them

Your soul is like a diamond. When you do not acknowledge and release your feelings, it's like wrapping a blanket over your soul. The more you avoid your feelings, the more it will fade until you can no longer see it. A counselor I saw years ago stated this to me. I never forgot what he told me, and I live by this statement every day by taking the time to acknowledge my feelings so they are aligned with the present.

Once you allow yourself to feel your painful feelings, they will be released and eventually disappear. Once you feel a specific feeling, acknowledge it in your mind, and find the source that provoked it. Once you have identified it, allow the feeling to pass through your body. You may feel your body tense up as your unconscious mind tries to block you from sensing the painful ones. Continue to focus on the feeling, and allow it to surface. Express the feeling according to what you are sensing:

- If you feel extremely sad, release it by allowing yourself to cry.
- If you feel angry, release it by punching a pillow.
- If you feel an urge to laugh, release it by laughing and so forth.

Releasing your feelings in this fashion will help keep your emotional states current so that feelings stemming from your past do not conflict with the present.

Turning Negative Feelings into Positive Ones

Encountering abusive behaviors will damage your spirit and cause you to experience low feelings such as unworthiness, inadequacy, loneliness, depression, thoughts of unimportance, and so forth. They can continue long after your relationship ends. You may find this hard to believe, but your mate's abusive behavior has nothing to do with you. It's based on past issues that do not involve you.

You do not need to hold on to these negative feelings because they are undeserving to you. You did nothing wrong to bear them. Your abusive mate may unconsciously project his underlying feelings and insecurities by causing you to experience them. Don't allow yourself to feel your abuser's feelings of low self-worth.

The negative feelings you have experienced actually originated in your mate. Causing you to experience them won't make them go away. Your mate may need counseling to deal with his feelings in a constructive way. Don't feel bad about yourself because of your abuser's behavior. Remember, you have nothing to feel bad about because the abuse is about a problem with him, not you!

Your mate's projected feelings do not belong within you. Let go of these negative feelings, and replace them with the positive ones you deserve. One way to help yourself sort out your feelings is to write them down and record the source that provoked these feelings. Identify if this feeling is truly relevant to you. For example:

1. What is the feeling?
2. Did you or your mate provoke the feeling?
3. Is the feeling relevant to you? Did you bear it because of something you did, or did something your mate said or did provoke it?

Finally, let the undeserving feelings go! Sorting out your feelings in this matter can help you see if your feelings are relevant to you. If you find that something your mate said or did provoked them, let go of them.

Reclaiming Your Trust

An abusive mate will take away the trust you had for others and yourself to prevent you from empowering yourself. By causing you to doubt yourself, he will cause you to lose your inner trust and the confidence you need to empower yourself. Once he takes away your inner trust, he has taken away your inner power.

An abuser feels dominant only when he takes away your power. Don't move on thinking that you no longer have power just because your abuser temporarily took it away. Your higher power gave you gifts at birth. You have eyes to see and ears to hear, a nose to smell, and a mouth to taste. You have feelings that you can sense emotionally as well as physically. You also have intuition and a mind that processes the information from what you see, hear, smell, taste, and feel.

These are spiritual gifts from your higher power. These gifts are your power, and they were given to you at birth so you could utilize them to protect yourself. If you do not, you will become vulnerable. For example, if you block the information from what your eyes see, you may trip over a stone and fall. If you block the information that came from your nose, you may not escape a burning building, and if you avoid your intuition, you could encounter emotional or physical pain and so forth.

It is important for you to trust and rely on your inner power. Your eyes, ears, nose, and feelings are powerful gifts that were given to you so you could guide and protect yourself. You need to be able to trust the information your inner gifts are conveying to you. You need to acknowledge and utilize your inner power and allow it to guide you. Your power is still within you. Trust and use your inner power to free yourself from the abuse.

Preventing Isolation

An abusive mate will violate your trust and take away the faith you had for others, including your family and friends. By giving you reasons not to trust them, he will cause you to isolate yourself from those who can help you and cause you to experience better. Isolating yourself is also damaging to your spirit.

Your family and friends will help heal your broken spirit. This is why your abuser isolated you from them in the first place. Surround yourself with family and friends. You need their support. Go see a funny movie with your friends. Laughter is known to be one of the best remedies for healing your emotional and physical health.

Dealing with Feelings of Low Self-Esteem

Being in an abusive relationship will lower your self-esteem to the point where you may actually believe that you are not worthy of anything better. Your confidence will surely disappear if you are involved with an abusive mate. He will lower your self-esteem to prevent you from leaving.

If you find yourself doubting your talents and abilities, engage in a hobby that you enjoy or work on a small, obtainable goal. Reaching your goal will surely boost your self-esteem. Isolation and feelings of low self-esteem can also make you feel inadequate around others. You will be surprised at how others respond to you when you are among them and will realize that you are not as bad as your abusive mate made you out to be, which will turn your feelings of inadequacy into ones of confidence.

Staying Connected

An abusive relationship can take your focus away from yourself to the point where you can no longer define yourself. You must stay connected with yourself because, when you lose the association, you are not able to utilize your inner power and will look to others to define yourself. For example, meditation will help keep you connected. Choose a time and place where you will not be distracted. Close your eyes, and start focusing on your breathing. With your eyes closed, visualize your physical appearance from your head down to your toes. Look at your hair, face, arms, legs, and feet. Now focus on the feelings passing through your body. Does your body feel at ease, or is it tense?

Acknowledge the thoughts that are passing through your mind. What are you thinking? Now connect with your identity, and answer these questions. Who are you? What are you about? What are you passionate about? Next, connect with your spirit. What are you feeling at this moment? Are you feeling peaceful, depressed, or happy? If your mind, body, and spirit are not in harmony, find out why, and then address the problem so they are in harmony.

Protecting Your Mind, Body, and Spirit

Take the time to nurture your mind, body, and spirit. Care for yourself as you attend to others. You can nurture your spirit by giving yourself what you need by paying close attention to your senses—for example, watching for the information your senses are sending you and then attending to them. Additionally:

- When you are feeling down, do something positive to change the feeling by watching a funny movie or playing with your pet.
- If you are feeling tired, give your body rest.
- If you are feeling lonely, go out to dinner with a friend.

You do not need to rely solely on others to feel love. You can experience love by nurturing yourself. Engage in things that bring you joy. Take part in a hobby, or sign up with some friends and go to a gym. Participating in things can be therapeutic and help you speed up the healing process.

Do not enter into another relationship too soon. Take the time to nurture yourself so you can experience love by giving it to yourself. Entering a relationship too soon can set you back into accepting less than what you deserve, especially if your self-esteem isn't up to par. Set boundaries for yourself, and avoid those who violate them. Stay clear of negative people. They will only bring you down. Stay with positive people who lift your spirit.

IN CLOSING

Unfortunately, we can encounter negative experiences in our relationships, even when we have done our best to prevent them. We may endlessly search inside of ourselves, looking for valid reasons as to why we encounter these experiences. Unfortunately, we may never know the motives. Encountering an abusive mate may cause you to feel deeply betrayed, especially when you have positively dedicated yourself to your relationship. These experiences may cause you to reevaluate your beliefs and possibly change them, which may prevent you from entering another relationship, thinking you will be robbed of the rewards if you dedicate yourself to them.

Trust is necessary in all relationships, whether it's a personal or business connection. Unfortunately, people will take advantage of our trust, but it's even more heartbreaking when a family member, friend, or intimate partner violates it. I have learned that our trust can be violated even when we are dedicated to our relationships. We place our trust in others, assuming they will be as trustworthy to us as we are to them. Placing our faith in our partners, however, does not guarantee that they will be trustworthy.

I have learned that it is up to us to know if we can trust our partners. Unfortunately, their words alone are not enough to prove their trustworthiness. We must look beyond their words to prove it to ourselves. Sometimes, we get caught up in life, trust the spoken words of our partners, and overlook their actions. We need to become more aware of their actions because their actions determine if they are trustworthy. We need to continuously watch their actions to see if they are in sync with their words. As the saying goes, actions speak louder than words! How true it is!

From my experiences, I have learned that trust must be the main focus in all of our relationships. We must continuously pay attention to other people's actions in order to know if they will remain honorable. We also need to have faith in ourselves. We need to trust our senses and allow them to guide us. Our senses are gifts from our higher power, which can guide us out of danger.

Do not allow your experiences to prevent you from living the life that you deserve. Once you regain your self-esteem and inner trust, I hope you will never lose them. I hope the information found throughout this book will help you identify the personality traits of an abusive mate so you can avoid the negative impact his behaviors can have on your life. I hope this book has given you clarity, understanding, empathy, and compassion so you can move forward by giving yourself the love that you deserve.

RECOMMENDATIONS

- *Why Does He Do That* by Lundy Bancroft, September 2003
- *No Visible Wounds* by Mary Susan Miller, PhD, October 1996
- *Boundaries* by Henry Cloud, May 1995
- *The Verbally Abusive Relationship* by Patricia Evans, January 2010
- *Survivors Speak Out* by Patricia Evans, February 2003
- *The Verbally Abusive Man* by Patricia Evans, October 2006
- *Controlling People* by Patricia Evans, February 2003
- *Life Code* by Dr. Phil, April 2013

Recommended Websites

- www.womansavers.com is a very informative site that empowers women. Women post information and pictures of their problem men on this site to warn other women.
- www.dontdatehimgirl.com is another informative site that empowers women. Women are also posting information and pictures of problem men on this site to warn other women.
- www.ncadv.org—The National Coalition against Domestic Violence is a non-profit organization that focuses on raising awareness about and preventing domestic violence.

ABOUT THE AUTHOR

Sharon Walsh Cook resides in the state of Pennsylvania. She has experienced domestic abuse in her past relationships, and a man she didn't know stalked her for nearly six years. She has written *Emotionally Abusive Husbands and Boyfriends* to help other women identify the less obvious forms of abusive behaviors so they can avoid the damaging effects that these behaviors cause.

Made in the USA
San Bernardino, CA
15 October 2014